Ethereum

————— ❧❦❧ —————

A Comprehensive Guide For Ethereum And How To Make Money With It

Mark Smith

Additionally, the information in the following pages is intended only for informational purposes and should thus be thought of as universal. As befitting its nature, it is presented without assurance regarding its prolonged validity or interim quality. Trademarks that are mentioned are done without written consent and can in no way be considered an endorsement from the trademark holder.

Table of Contents

Introduction

These days, it may seem like every time you open your computer, there is an ad or some kind of feed regarding Ethereum or its virtual currency, the Ether. Many people have heard of Ethereum and its counterpart, the Ether, but few people understand what Ethereum actually is. This ebook is designed to answer your questions about what Ethereum is and how it works.

Ethereum was created by a Russian-Canadian teenager named Vitalik Buterin. It is basically a blockchain on which developers can create a particular kind of app known as a decentralized application, or Dapp. Its underlying genius is the use of something called the smart contract, a contract written in code that is enforced without the use of a third-party mediator. The Ether is the currency used to power the Ethereum network.

This ebook will guide you through all of the basics of Ethereum. It will begin by explaining in more detail what Ethereum is and what smart contracts are. It will then explain what blockchain technology is and how blockchain is used in the Ethereum network. After that, it will show you what Gas and Ether are and how they work. Next, it will go through some applications that run on Ethereum to help give you a feel for what kind of apps Ethereum is best-suited for. Finally, it will give you some ideas for how you can make money on Ethereum.

Ethereum

If you are ready to understand what Ethereum is and how you can make money on it, then this ebook is definitely for you!

Chapter 1:

What is Ethereum?

Vitalik Buterin and the Founding of Ethereum

Vitalik Buterin was born in Kolomna, a city near Moscow in Russia, in the year 1994. His father was a computer programmer, and his mother was a business analyst. When he was six years old, his family moved to Canada in search of employment opportunities and a better life. As a young child, Buterin quickly discovered his interest in mathematics and its applications in computer programming; in fact, he was a mathematical genius. He was able to quickly add large sums in his head, something that not only most young children but even adults have difficulty doing.

When Bitcoin was first released in 2009, Buterin was only 15 years old. Two years later, when Bitcoin was beginning to gain some traction, his father introduced him to it. He became the co-founder of *Bitcoin Magazine*, and was also one of its primary contributing writers; he remained there until the middle of 2014. He also wrote about Bitcoin in other publications, including the scholarly, peer-reviewed publication *Ledger*, which provides information on blockchain and cryptocurrencies.

Ethereum

In 2013, when Buterin was 19 years old, he went to a conference on cryptocurrency in San Jose. While some considered cryptocurrency to be another pending dotcom boom and bust, Buterin decided that the movement was real and he wanted to be a part of it. He was in school at the University of Waterloo, but he dropped out to pursue Bitcoin interests.

When Buterin returned home to Toronto, he wrote a white paper on a new blockchain idea that he called Ethereum. In June 2014, he was awarded a $100,000 Peter Thiel Fellowship, which he used to develop Ethereum.

The idea immediately took off and was an instant success. Ethereum quickly became seen as an alternative to Bitcoin, and Buterin was featured in Fortune's 40 Under 40 list.

The Ethereum Network

Ethereum is an open-source network that is built using blockchain technology (for more information on what blockchain is and how it works, see the next chapter). It enables individuals, businesses, and other entities to develop their own decentralized applications.

Dapps. A decentralized application, also known as a Dapp, is a new concept that works differently than traditional applications, such as Gmail or most online banking websites. These traditional applications are centralized, meaning that they are connected to one main server. If that one main server fails, the entire network will fail. Furthermore, the server acts as a type of "middleman" that all transactions must go through in order to be processed. Because a Dapp is decentralized, there is no main server to process transactions. Rather, it is open-source, meaning that anyone is able to access the code.

Further, no one person is able to hold a majority share of the application, so any changes made to it must be by a popular consensus of the Dapp's users.

According to the white paper that Vitalik Buterin published for Ethereum, a Dapp must meet five conditions. It must A) be open-source and autonomous so that no one person or entity controls the majority of it, B) have any protocol changes agreed upon by all users, C) store all of its information in a public blockchain, D) use a cryptocurrency native to the blockchain on which the Dapp operates (meaning that a Dapp that is built onto the Bitcoin blockchain must operate using Bitcoins, and a Dapp that is built onto the Ethereum blockchain must operate using Ether), and E) must generate cryptocurrency tokens using a predetermined algorithm.

One example of a Dapp is Alice.SI, which holds charities accountable for actually making an impact by doing the charitable work that they claim to do. The Dapp works through smart contracts (see the section below on smart contracts) to ensure that donations to charities are only processed if the charity actually does the work it promises. Another Dapp is Coakt, which has taken crowdfunding beyond raising money to also raising talent and technology to support people's ideas and goals. In order to fully access many Dapps and use them to their full potential, users must use an Ethereum-compatible browser, such as Mist.

Dapps have their own advantages over traditional applications, and some have even said that they are the next step in the evolution of computer technology. One advantage is that because there is no centralized server that Dapps connect to, there is no central point of failure; if one server that the Dapp connects to fails, there are plenty of other servers that will keep it running. Another advantage is that the applications are cryptographically secure inside a blockchain network. Therefore, they are inherently protected against things such as hacking and other fraudulent activities.

There are three main types of Dapps, with each type containing its own subtypes. The first type of Dapp has its own blockchain. Examples include networks such as Bitcoin, Ethereum, Litecoin, Lysk, and other networks that run on their own cryptocurrencies. The second type of Dapp is built onto a blockchain and runs similarly to a software program. It runs on its own rules and protocols and uses the tokens of the blockchain onto which it is embedded. The third type of Dapp is built onto the second type of Dapp to develop a more specialized type of software. Each type of Dapp serves a different purpose and provides a different type of contribution to the people that it serves.

In his white paper, Buterin proposed three types of Dapps that would be powered by the Ethereum network. The first type would power financial applications and provide the users with trustless ways of managing their money and processing transactions. Examples include things such as savings wallets, cryptocurrency exchanges, wills, and even some employment contracts. The second type would be for semi-financial applications; a semi-financial application is one in which money is exchanged but most of what is involved is not monetary. The third type is what Buterin called "Governance Applications," and refers to applications that do not involve any kind of financial transaction. These applications can be used for functions such as voting in governmental elections and providing decentralized governance.

In many ways, Dapps are still in their infancy. The concept is still being explored by programmers, and some innovators are looking for new ways to exploit the technology to further revolutionize how computing can be made safer and more secure in this digital and information age. Applications such as online voting are still a long way away, and the general public is not fully aware of what Dapps are and how they can be beneficial over traditional apps. As Ethereum gains more traction in the coming years, the full potential of Dapps will undoubtedly be more fully explored.

DAO's. Buterin also envisioned that Ethereum would enable and support the creation and use of DAO's. A DAO is a Decentralized Autonomous Organization that can be used to handle financial transactions without any middleman or breach of trust. Rather than being a brick-and-mortar company, it is entirely embedded in computer code.

DAO's are notoriously hard to define because they can exist in a multitude of forms. As a general principle, though, they function as digital ledgers that are timestamped embedded in a blockchain. Therefore, they are next to impossible to alter and must be carried out. For more information on how this works, see the section on Smart Contracts and the chapter on Blockchain.

The DAO was a company designed to leverage the use of DAO's and was built into the Ethereum blockchain in 2016. However, a weakness in the code used to create it was exploited, and $55 million dollars was siphoned off the network. In response, Ethereum created a hard fork in its network to help restore the viability of the blockchain and replace the funds that had been lost.

Smart Contracts. Smart contracts are a concept that was initially envisioned by Nick Szabo in 1996. Nick Szabo arguably came up with the concept of cryptocurrency over a decade before Satoshi Nakamoto created Bitcoin in 2008-

2009, and some believe that he may actually be the legendary figure. Smart contracts are, in some ways, an extension or natural evolution of the blockchain technology that was used to create Bitcoin and later Ethereum. In fact, they are largely used in facilitating the exchange of cryptocurrencies.

A smart contract is a computer protocol that is intended to create and enforce the execution of financial and other transactions. It is extremely similar to a DAO in many ways. When two parties agree to enter into a smart contract, the terms of the contract become embedded as a block in the blockchain. The block is timestamped, and because more blocks are subsequently added to the blockchain, going back to retroactively change the smart contract is impossible (for more information on how blockchain works, see the chapter on Blockchain). Furthermore, that block becomes publicly visible; instead of a middleman, such as an escrow service, ensuring that the terms of the contract are carried out, the entire network of users on the blockchain serve as witnesses to the contract's veracity. However, the identities of the people involved in the contract remain anonymous. When both parties have completed their duties and the terms of the contract are fulfilled, the smart contract releases whatever has been held.

For example, imagine that Bob and Joe want to exchange Bitcoin. Bob has one Bitcoin that he wants to sell for $4000, and Joe agrees to buy it. They draw up a smart contract, and according to its terms, they have one day (exactly 24 hours, at which time the smart contract will expire) to complete the transaction. Bob transfers the Bitcoin into the smart contract, and Joe transfers in the $4000. At the end of the 24 hours, the smart contract releases the $4000 to Bob and the one Bitcoin to Joe.

In many ways, smart contracts are the driving vehicle behind the Ethereum network. Their trusty nature and complete anonymity has drawn many people to Ethereum, and many of the Dapps on the Ethereum network function largely by using smart contracts.

Ethereum vs Bitcoin

Ethereum has been described by some as a rival to Bitcoin. After all, its digital token, the Ether, soared in value — by over 4000% — just in the first half of 2017! Bitcoin has long dominated the cryptocurrency scene, and has also grown substantially in the year 2017. However, some anticipate that the value of the Ether may surpass that of Bitcoin over the next few years.

There are some key differences between Ethereum and Bitcoin. Satoshi Nakamoto's concept of Bitcoin was the impetus behind his invention of blockchain technology, and Vitalik Buterin worked extensively with the Bitcoin community before creating Ethereum. The biggest difference is that Ethereum was not primarily designed for the creation, distribution, and facilitation of the Ether cryptocurrency. Rather, it was designed to enable entities to develop Dapps onto the blockchain. The Ether was created to help enable the execution of the Dapps (for more information on how the Ether works, see the chapter on Gas and Ether). Bitcoin, however, was not created to power a network. It was created exclusively as a cryptocurrency. In other words, Ethereum is a network for computer programs, while Bitcoin is exclusively a cryptocurrency. Therefore, the Ether is connected to an actual "product," while Bitcoin exists entirely autonomously.

The next few chapters will better explain some of the mechanics behind how Ethereum works, including what

Ethereum

blockchain technology is, how Ethereum uses it, and how the Ether works.

Chapter 2:

Blockchain

Blockchain is the technology behind the creation of cryptocurrencies, most notably Bitcoin, and was used by Buterin to create Ethereum. Buterin realized that while blockchain was created for Bitcoin, its uses went far beyond cryptocurrency.

The concept was initially laid out in Satoshi Nakamoto's white paper on Bitcoin, which was published on October 31, 2008. The technology was actually developed as a means of facilitating the cryptocurrency that Nakamoto envisioned. To better explain how blockchain works, this chapter will take a historical look at how the ideas that lead to the development of the technology evolved into the powerful networks used today.

History of Blockchain

During the 1980s, computer technology advanced to the point where many entities were using software that allowed altering and modification of photographs; the growing, extensive use of this software raised questions about how to protect data and sensitive information from tampering and how to ensure that it had not been altered. Two computer programmers, Stuart Haber and Scott Stornetta, proposed a solution that they published in an article entitled "How to Time-Stamp a Digital

Document," which was published in the *Journal of Cryptology*. Their solution was that rather than timestamping documents, business should timestamp the actual data that is transacted. The method that they proposed would ensure that the data contained in a digital document could not be modified. Their method was the foundation of blockchain's digital-ledger feature, which prohibits the altering of data in transactions.

A few years later and into the 2000s, a Cambridge University expert in cybersecurity named Ross Anderson advocated the need for a paradigm shift in how computer security works. Current computer security models were extremely vulnerable to security breaches and hacks; infamously, many hacks were directed at government and military servers, and some hacks directed at commercial companies siphoned off millions dollars and exposed personal information of many customers and clients. The need for an entirely new model of cybersecurity was an important impetus behind the creation of blockchain, which did not build on other models of computer security but rather created an entirely new paradigm.

More innovative ideas continued to come from leaders in computer programming. At the time, they did not revolutionize programming, but they continued to lay the foundation for the eventual creation of blockchain. For example, in 1998 a programmer named Michael Doyle filed for a patent that would create new security protocols using chain-of-evidence protocols, along with public and private keys to ensure that the data being transacted was not subject to tampering. His system ensured that data was accurately timestamped without any need for third-party verification. The system that he developed helped create blockchain's trustless feature, which refers to the fact that no trust in a third party or middle man is required for someone to make a transaction on the blockchain.

The same year that Michael Doyle filed for his patent, Nick Szabo, an expert in digital contractual law, developed a model for a digital currency that he referred to as "bit gold." Users would solve complex mathematical problems to "mine" the cryptocurrency, and the solutions to those problems would be used to create the next set of problems. Bit gold was never actually developed, but the methods that Szabo proposed developed the concept of a peer-to-peer network. A peer-to-peer network is one in which users must collaborate with each other rather than rely on a centralized entity to confirm transactions. The peer-to-peer network is an essential feature of blockchain, as it is the primary way of enforcing the trustworthiness of the network.

Three men named Charles Bry, Vladimir Oksman, and Neal Kin filed for a patent in August of 2008 for a new encryption technology that they had developed. This technology would require the use of public and private keys — as conceived of by Michael Doyle ten years earlier — to encrypt the information that was being transacted. The patent was for an almost exact model of blockchain, but all three men deny any connection to the mysterious Satoshi Nakamoto.

On October 31, 2008, an individual writing under the pseudonym of Satoshi Nakamoto published a white paper about his conception of using cryptocurrency. He named his cryptocurrency Bitcoin, an amalgam of "bit," referring to the unit used in computer science, and "coin." The name alluded to the fact that it was to be a currency that would exist entirely in a digital form rather than being printed as cash or minted as coins. In January of 2009, Nakamoto released Bitcoin and with it, the blockchain technology that sustained the network.

Ethereum

As previously mentioned, blockchain was developed originally for the creation of Bitcoin. However, its uses go far beyond Bitcoin, as Vitalik Buterin realized when he decided to create Ethereum.

How Blockchain Works

Blockchain is an entirely different method of computer programming. It did not improve on previous models but rather created a new paradigm for both programming and security.

Traditional computing models have an application that connects directly to a central server. For example, if you want to make an online purchase from a retailer whose online platform uses the traditional model, your transaction will have to pass through a central server. If the central server has failed for whatever reason — maybe there is too much web traffic or it is being worked on — your transaction will not be completed, and you will have to try again later. If your bank uses the traditional model for its online services and you want to access your financial information online, if the central server has failed, you will be unable to accomplish your goal. Not being able to access your bank information when you need it, especially in this increasingly digitized world, can have catastrophic consequences for your personal finances. Furthermore, the traditional model is extremely susceptible to hacking. A hacker merely needs to get into the central server, and then all of the information contained in that application is at his or her disposal. This information can include vast amounts of money, credit card and bank account information, social security numbers, and numerous other pieces of compromising and vulnerable personal information. As you may be able to see, the traditional model is outdated and not secure, as Ross Anderson took great pains to point out.

The blockchain model does not rely on a centralized server but rather an entire network of hundreds, if not thousands, of users who power the network. These users are able to verify the transactions that have occurred; in fact, a critical number of users are required to verify transactions before they are completed. This decentralized model has several implications. One is that the network is not controlled by any one person or entity but rather by the people who use the network. Another is that the network is virtually impenetrable to hackers, as in order to gain access to the network, every single user would have to be in conclusion to bring it down.

Below are some of the features of blockchain; understanding these features will help you understand the mechanics of how blockchain works.

Public ledger. At its core, blockchain is essentially a public ledger. A ledger is a collection of transactions that have occurred, usually kept by an accountant. Ledgers may be kept in software programs such as Quick Books and only be visible to authorized persons, such as the accountant, CEO, and any auditing service. Other interested parties, such as shareholders and employees, may not have access to the ledger and therefore be unaware of the company's financial health. Secrecy about the company ledger was a critical factor in the 2000 collapse of Enron, which caused many people to lose all of their money.

As a public ledger, anyone on the blockchain is able to view the transactions that have occurred or that are in process, albeit with anonymity regarding the parties involved in the transactions. Therefore, no one person is able to alter the data in any way.

Each transaction that occurs is recorded in a block. When a new transaction occurs, it is recorded in a block that is connected to the previous one. The connected blocks together form a chain, hence the "blockchain." This is why blockchain is essentially a ledger, and because it is visible to the public, it is a public ledger. In order to change the data contained in one of the blocks, one would not only need the collusion of every single user on the network but would also have to retroactively change every single block that comes after the block to be changed.

In Ethereum, each smart contract occurs as a block in the blockchain. Therefore, the terms of the contract must be carried out by the parties involved, and no one is able to retroactively change the contract.

Nodes. A node is a client computer on a blockchain network that processes and verifies transactions. Rather than one centralized server, blockchains usually have hundreds, if not thousands of nodes, which are usually operated on a volunteer basis. Some blockchains, such as Bitcoin, are seeing the number of nodes on their networks decline; to help solve this problem, Bitcoin is making plans to put nodes in outer space!

Peer-to-peer network. Because a blockchain network is decentralized, instead of a central authority regulating it the users themselves are the authority. They must work together and agree upon the transactions that have occurred, whether those transactions involve exchanges of cryptocurrency, mining (to be explained later in this section), or the execution of a smart contract. If the users on the network do not agree on a transaction, it is considered to be invalid.

As previously explained, the peer-to-peer network inherently provides such a high degree of cybersecurity that it is virtually impervious to any hacks or data tampering.

Timestamps. A timestamp is a record of the exact time at which a transaction occurred. They are essential in business and legal environments because they ensure that certain data existed at a particular time. One ubiquitous use of timestamps is the practice of clocking in for work. Businesses usually have an established protocol to ensure that employees are at work at a certain time so that they can be compensated accordingly. Tampering with timestamps can cause serious legal ramifications.

Blockchain technology relies on the use of timestamps to ensure the authenticity of transactions and utilizes Satoshi Nakamoto's method for ensuring that the timestamps are tamper-proof. As soon as a transaction occurs and a block with the transaction's data is created, that block is timestamped before becoming permanently embedded within the blockchain. The timestamp cannot be changed unless the entire network decides to make the change and every single block in the blockchain that has been created after that transaction is also changed. While there is presently no legal precedent, the consensus seems to be that a blockchain timestamp will hold up in a court of law.

Public and private keys. Public key cryptography is an essential blockchain feature because it helps prevent any fraudulent transactions from occurring. Users on a blockchain network have both a public key and a private key; the public key is visible to anyone, but the private key must be kept absolutely secret. When one user wants to make a transaction with another user, he or she will use that person's public key to send the transaction. The sender's private key will be used to encrypt the transaction so that it cannot be received by anyone except the intended recipient. The recipient will use his or her private key to open the message.

If a user's private key was to be exposed, someone would be able to access that person's account and make transactions. In the case of virtual currency, such as Bitcoin and Ether, the private key could be used to siphon off the person's entire holdings.

Hashes. Hashes are an important part of the blockchain's verification protocol. A hash takes a mathematical input of any size, runs it through an algorithm, and returns an output of a fixed size. The probability of any two hashes being the same is extremely low. Hashing is one way of keeping hackers from being able to access accounts on the blockchain. The following sections on proof-of-work and mining and forging will help you put the concept of hashing into the context of how it works in a blockchain.

Proof-of-work. A proof-of-work system is basically a method of proving that work was done to produce a transaction, meaning that the transaction was not made by bots. In a proof-of-work, a group of transactions are grouped together into a block, which is verified by a group of miners (see the below section on mining). The hash value from the preceding block is applied into an algorithm of the new block that is waiting to be verified, thereby creating a complex mathematical problem for miners to solve. The first miner to solve the problem is usually rewarded with a certain amount of cryptocurrency. In the Bitcoin blockchain, the difficulty of each block's problem is adjusted so that only one block can be solved (or mined) every 10 minutes. When the problem has been solved, the transactions inside the block are considered to be verified.

Ethereum has found that the proof-of-work system is extremely costly, both in terms of time and energy, so it has designed a new protocol called proof-of-stake. Proof-of-stake has the same goal and outcome as proof-of-work (ensuring that all transactions are legitimate), but it functions through a different process. There is no reward for the miners; rather, they take the transaction fees that are included in each Ether transaction. In a proof-of-stake protocol, the hash from the previous block is still applied into an algorithm. However, instead of miners competing to solve the complex mathematical problem that is generated, the creator of the new block (i.e., the miner who solved the problem) is chosen randomly based on the amount of wealth (i.e., stake) that that person has.

Mining and Forging. Mining is the process whereby new coins of the cryptocurrency used by the blockchain are created. It was developed by Satoshi Nakamoto as part of his proof-of-work protocol. Miners compete with each other to solve the complex mathematical problems that are created during the proof-of-work process. When the problem is solved, the block is considered to be mined. A set number of Bitcoins are released into circulation, with the miner receiving a portion of them as a reward.

Because Ethereum uses proof-of-stake instead of proof-of-work, it uses a process that is referred to as forging (referring to the process that blacksmiths use to create a new metal-based piece). Forging is similar to mining, except that new Ether tokens are not created when a block is solved. Rather, there is a fixed amount of Ether in circulation. While miners take a commission of the virtual currency that is created, forgers only take the transaction fees.

Ethereum virtual machine. Every time an Ethereum transaction is performed, thousands of node computers in the Ethereum network must collaborate in order to process the transaction. The transaction is written into a smart contract, which is then translated into a bytecode. The bytecode is read by the computers in the network using the Ethereum virtual machine, or EVM. Essentially, the EVM is a program used to interpret the bytecode. The EVM and miners running the nodes reject smart contracts that have not been paid for and ensure that no one is able to spend the same Ether twice.

Benefits of blockchain. Perhaps the most obvious benefit of blockchain is its security. Because of the peer-to-peer nature of a blockchain network, it cannot be hacked. All of the data on the blockchain is visible to everyone in the network because it actually relies on the people in the network, rather than a centralized authority (such as PayPal or MasterCard) to verify the transactions. This feature means that the network is transparent; there is no question about whether financial information is being recorded accurately and ethically. Another benefit of blockchain is that the data cannot be manipulated in any way; again, this is because there is no centralized authority. Any attempt at tampering with the data or manipulating the protocols would have to require the consensus of the blockchain's entire community!

Challenges of blockchain. While the benefits of blockchain cannot be understated, there are some challenges associated with it that will need to be met in the coming years to ensure its viability. One such challenge is how blockchain transactions should be viewed in a court of law. Because the technology is relatively new, as of right now there are few legal precedents regarding how the data in blockchain should be viewed legally. Another challenge is the energy required to run a blockchain network. Because hundreds, if not thousands, of computers are required to run the network, the carbon footprint created by blockchains is enormous. Estimates are that by the year 2020, Bitcoin will use as much energy as all of Denmark! One transaction on the Ethereum network uses as much energy as a typical family uses in a day and a half. This energy challenge can be met by providing incentives to users who use green energy to power their computers.

Another challenge associated with blockchain is the time required to complete a transaction. Because of the intense verification process, one Bitcoin transaction can take anywhere from 10 minutes to one hour. This can be a problem for users who want to use Bitcoin to buy a cup of coffee! Ethereum has met this challenge by establishing a new yet equally intense verification process, which has cut down the transaction time to about 12 seconds.

Chapter 3:

Blockchain and Ethereum

Like the Bitcoin concept that inspired the creation of Ethereum, all transactions made on the Ethereum network are part of the blockchain. The users are all linked together in the peer-to-peer network and collaborate with each other to make transactions.

How to Make an Ethereum Transaction

Before you can create a smart contract on Ethereum, the first thing that you need to do is create an account. Ethereum runs by using the Ether cryptocurrency (for more information, see the chapter on Gas and Ether), and all transactions require the use of Ether. This is to ensure that developers create strong codes and the people running the network are properly compensated. In order to use the Ethereum network, you may need the Mist Internet browser.

To create an account, you need to create a wallet that will allow you to store, send, and receive Ether. The wallet is like your gateway into the Ethereum network; in addition to managing your Ether, it allows you to write and execute smart contracts. First, you will need to download the wallet; this process will actually connect you to the entire Ethereum blockchain. Go to www.ethereum.org and scroll down the page until you see a link to download the Ethereum Mist Wallet. Clicking on this link will immediately begin to download the wallet as a zip file. You will need to unzip the file and then launch it.

After the launch is complete, you will be asked whether you want to use the test network or the main network. The test network is a sandbox; a sandbox is a program that runs only some of the computer's resources. This way, if a code on the program proves to be defective, only the resources used by the sandbox will be affected. The rest of the system will be unharmed. If you choose to use the test network, no Ether will be required. Use of the main network, however, will require Ether; the program will assist you in acquiring some.

Next, you will need to create a password. This password is used in creating your private key for sending and receiving transactions, so protecting it is of vital importance. Choose a strong password that other people will not be able to guess. Make absolutely certain that you remember your password, as it cannot ever be changed.

You will then be directed to your account's main page. At the top of the screen, you will see links labeled Send, Contracts, and Balance. You will also see in the middle how many nodes in the blockchain you are synced to. Below, you will see a bar that says Main Account. Below that is a string of numbers and letters; that is your public key, which is used by other people when sending you Ether.

To send Ether to someone, click the Send link at the top of the screen. Type in the public key of the person to whom you wish to send Ether and the amount that you wish to send. Next, you will be taken to a sliding scale to determine the maximum amount that the transaction will cost; this amount is paid to the miners who process the transaction. If you want to send the transaction as cheaply as possible, you will pay less but wait longer because with less money, the miners have less incentive to process your transaction. If you wish to send the transaction as quickly as possible, you will pay more but the transaction will be completed in just a few seconds. You will then enter your password to confirm this transaction; even though you must use your password to access your account, this feature adds in an extra layer of security.

How an Ethereum Transaction Works

A transaction on the Ethereum network can seem relatively straightforward to a user who is trying to exchange Ether or create a smart contract. However, the actual mechanics behind the transaction are actually quite complex. Here is an overview of what happens behind the scenes.

When making a transaction, the sender uses the public key of the intended recipient. Remember that the public key is visible to anyone; however, the private key (which is generated from the password) must be kept absolutely secret.

When the transaction is sent, the data becomes embedded in a block, which is connected to the block that came before it. It is now part of the blockchain, and is visible to everyone on the network, albeit without the identities of the users involved. The data in this transaction is included with data from other transactions in the block. The hash value from the preceding block is applied into a complex mathematical problem, which the miners (or forgers) must solve in order for the transactions to be verified. The solution is used to generate a hash value, which becomes applied to the next block in the blockchain. The miners are rewarded with the transaction fees that were paid by the senders.

Ethereum

The intended recipient will receive a notification that he or she has received Ether. He or she will log in to the account and receive the money.

Chapter 4:

Gas and Ether

The crucial difference between Bitcoin and Ethereum is that Bitcoin is a virtual currency and nothing more. It has an exceptionally high value that continues to increase and has shaken up concepts of what money is and how it should be regulated. However, it is not connected to an actual commodity. Think of it like gold: The price of gold is not connected to any particular good or service, and it is not as subject to things like inflation as standard currency, such as the dollar, is. Its value is based on how much people are willing to pay for it; in other words, the price of gold is determined by its demand. The demand for Bitcoin is high, so its value is also high.

Ethereum is not a virtual currency; rather, it is a commodity. It is a network that allows users to create and execute smart contracts, as well as develop their own Dapps. Running this network is rather costly; think of how much energy is required, considering that it is maintained by a system of thousands of node computers. Furthermore, there is a need to ensure that the Dapps created on the network are made efficiently and to the highest standards. Therefore, money is involved, ensuring that people are properly compensated for their work. That money comes in the form of Ether.

What is Gas?

Gas on Ethereum is similar to the gas that is required to run your car. The amount of gas that you need to put in your car is directly proportional to the amount of energy required for you to drive your car to your desired destination. If your car is a gas guzzler and you are making a cross-country trip (something that environmentalists would strongly advise against), a lot of energy will be consumed. Therefore, you will need a lot of gas. If you drive a Prius and are taking a weekend getaway to a beach that is two hours from your house, very little energy will be consumed, especially compared to the gas guzzler going across the country. Therefore, you will need much less gas.

Transactions on Ethereum take a lot of energy. They don't only require the energy required to power the computers on the network, but also the human energy required in the mining (or forging) process. After all, the miners need an incentive to process a transaction.

One thing that is important to note is that nobody owns Ethereum, not even the creator, Vitalik Buterin. The fees paid for gas do not go to fund a wealthy CEO's fourth vacation home. Rather, they pay for the workers on the network to do their jobs.

Some transactions on Ethereum, such as sending Ether, are relatively simple and straightforward. Other transactions, such as creating a new Dapp, are much more complex. Think of the simpler transactions as Prius cars and the more complex transactions as SUVs from the 1990s. A simple transaction requires less energy and therefore less gas. A more complex transaction requires significant amounts of energy and therefore a lot of gas.

One feature of gas in Ethereum is that the user gets to determine how much to pay for gas. While the amount of gas required to perform a transaction is the same (just as the amount of gas required to drive your car to a particular destination won't change), the amount of money that the user *pays* for the gas is up to him or her. Think of this scenario as different gas prices across the country; in some parts of the country, like California, gas is a lot more expensive than in places like the American South. Imagine being able to live in California while only paying as much for gas as someone in Mississippi! However, there is a catch.

When you send a transaction, you are given a sliding scale of how much you want to pay for gas. On one end is the cheapest option, which will usually take longer to process because, with less money involved, the miners have less incentive to process it. On the other end is the fastest option, which is more expensive but gives your transaction a priority spot inside its block. It is processed much faster because the miners have a higher incentive. If the transaction does not have enough gas, then like a car that runs out in the middle of the highway, the transaction stops before being processed.

How Does Gas Work?

Chapter 2 briefly explained the Ethereum Virtual Machine, or EVM. The EVM is basically a mechanism for running codes on the Ethereum network. It functions as a sandbox, meaning that it only uses a minimal amount of a computer's resources. Sandboxes are ideal environments for running test codes, because if there is a defect in the code (such as a virus), only the limited resources used by the sandbox will be affected. The EVM is used by developers to execute their test codes before they become integrated into the main Ethereum network.

In addition to testing codes, the EVM is an essential part of Ethereum's verification process. All transactions pass through the EVM, which is connected to every node on the Ethereum network. Think of the EVM as Ethereum's World Computer. Every operation on the World Computer uses gas; the amount of gas used is connected to the complexity of the operation involved. The fees from the gas go to pay the miners, to compensate them for their work in keeping the network going.

What is Ether?

When fueling up your car, you probably pay for the gas in dollars (or British pounds sterling, or Euros, or whatever fiat currency you use). When fueling up on Ethereum, you pay for the gas in Ether. Ether is the virtual currency tied to the Ethereum network. However, its soaring value has caused it to gain traction outside of Ethereum programmers, and even the mainstream media is picking up on this phenomenon. While Bitcoin is still the leader in the world of virtual currency, the Ether is growing at a faster rate. In fact, some analysts anticipate that within the next few years, the value of the Ether will surpass the value of Bitcoin!

Before explaining what makes the Ether unique, it may be helpful to fully understand what cryptocurrencies are. First, you need to understand what currency is. While many people like to think of currency as the dollars and cents that they use to pay for things, it is much more than that. Currency is a *medium of exchange*. In other words, anything that you have that I agree can be exchanged for something that I have is a currency. If you have a Snickers bar and I have a Mars bar, yet you want the Mars bar, you can ask me if you can trade the Snickers for Mars. If I agree, then the Snickers has become the currency that you used to obtain the Mars.

This concept is very, very old; in fact, some archaeologists and anthropologists suggest that the use of currency is what defined the advent of human civilization. In ancient cultures, trading often occurred between people so that goods could be shared across the population. For example, a potter could trade his or her pottery with a farmer in exchange for food. In that case, the pottery became the currency, or the medium of exchange. Furthermore, people often traveled by land or sea to trade with other cultures. Whatever was agreed upon as a meaningful exchange became the currency used in the trade.

How was the value of currency determined? Well, largely by the individual people involved. If you wanted to buy clothes from me and pay for them using peacock feathers, but I had no use for peacock feathers, they would be worthless to me; therefore, I would not agree to the trade. However, if you wanted to pay for them in silver beads, and I knew that I could use those silver beads to buy something from somebody else, then that currency would have value to me. It would become the medium with which we would exchange our goods.

One feature of centralized governments is that the government became the regulating body of currency. In the United States, the dollar is minted by the US Treasury and, with some exceptions, is the only currency accepted as money. Currencies that are regulated by a central regulating body are known as fiat currencies. "Fiat" means "faith," and refers to the fact that use of the currency is not based on the intrinsic value of the paper used in the dollar (which is pretty close to worthless) but based on faith in the government that issued it. The government backs the currency and guarantees that it will not fail.

The value of the dollar is regulated by the government. It sets interest rates meant to raise or lower the dollar's value;

therefore, however much money you may have in dollars, the value of that money is determined by the government.

This regulating concept is actually an abnormality in the basic laws of supply and demand, which define many modern economic theories. Usually, when something is in high demand, its value goes up because people become willing to pay more money for it. When something is in low demand, its value goes down because people aren't willing to pay as much for it. The value of the dollar (and many other fiat currencies, as well) is not determined by the demand for it but rather by what the government says its value is. In other words, the value of the dollar is artificial.

But what if there was a currency whose value was determined by popular demand? Think back to how currency used to function: simply as a medium of exchange that one party was willing to accept in return for its goods. Its value was determined by the people involved in the transaction, not by a centralized government that artificially determined what it was worth. That is the concept behind virtual currency, or cryptocurrency, as some call it.

Cryptocurrency is not regulated by any central government or regulating body; therefore, it is decentralized. Its value is not set by any individual but rather is determined by the people who use the currency, based on the laws of supply and demand.

This concept was behind the creation of Bitcoin, the first cryptocurrency. The creator, Satoshi Nakamoto, envisioned a currency that put power back into the hands of the people rather than fueling the government's own interests. Nearly ten years after Bitcoin's inception, even though the United States government has made many attempts to regulate it, it is still unregulated. Rather than being a liability, this lack of regulation has proven to be possibly Bitcoin's greatest asset. Popular demand of Bitcoin has skyrocketed, and in turn, so has its value. Its value has never been falsely inflated or deflated to reflect the caprices and whims of its governing body but rather is entirely linked to the demand that people have for it. Because of this, it is actually a truer currency than the dollar.

Vitalik Buterin, the creator of Ethereum, worked with the Bitcoin community for a few years before going rogue and creating his own blockchain. The idea of the Ether stems from that of Bitcoin, but with a crucial difference: While Bitcoin is not tied to any particular commodity, the Ether is. Ether is used to power the Ethereum network, so anyone who wants to use Ethereum must invest in Ether.

Like other cryptocurrencies, Ether does not exist in a physical form as cash. Rather, it is essentially a code. Ether has several different uses, which are outlined below.

Pay for gas. One use of Ether is to pay for gas, thereby enabling users to make a transaction on Ethereum. As previously explained, the amount of gas required to make a transaction is set, but the cost of the gas is determined by the user making the transaction. A sliding scale is shown, on which the user selects how much he or she wants to pay for gas. Paying more for gas makes that transaction a priority for the miners, who receive the fee as their compensation.

Invest. The value of the Ether has skyrocketed, going up 4500% just in the first half of 2017! This surge is due to increased use of the Ethereum network and therefore higher demand for the Ether. Major companies, such as JP Morgan and Merck, are beginning to experiment with Ethereum, meaning that they are also now making some exchanges in Ether.

In terms of investing, virtual currencies are far from a certain bet. They are historically known to be exceptionally volatile; now, with major investors joining the Ethereum market, there are concerns that the price could continue to surge before plummeting. Some individual projects that use Ether are now valued at hundreds of millions of dollars; if those projects should fail, they could potentially take the Ether market down with them.

Nevertheless, depending on your investment and other financial goals, Ether may prove to be a great use of your investment funds. When making any investment, but especially in cryptocurrency, the best rule of thumb is to only invest what you are willing to lose.

In order to invest in Ether, you will need to get a virtual currency wallet. A wallet functions much the same as your bank account's online service; you log in to your account and see a ledger of your transaction history.

There are several different types of wallets, and whichever one you choose should be the one that will best help you meet your goals. All types of virtual currency wallets are classified as either hot or cold. A hot wallet is one that operates online, meaning that it is always connected to the Internet. These wallets are the easiest for hackers to access, so storing large amounts of cryptocurrency in them is not recommended. Hot wallets are best suited for people who engage in frequent trading and therefore need ongoing access to their wallets. A cold wallet is one that operates offline on the user's computer desktop; the only way for hackers to access it is for them to first access the desktop. Cold storage is best for long-term investing and holding larger amounts of cryptocurrency.

Coinbase is the most popular wallet for buying and trading Ether. Make sure that the wallet you choose trades in Ether. Usually, you can buy Ether directly from the wallet. You purchase the Ether using fiat currency — usually dollars, but other currencies, such as pounds and Euros, may be accepted as well — based on the current exchange rate. For example, if the current value of Ether is $400, then you will pay $400 to purchase one Ether. You can also purchase portions of an Ether by choosing to pay a set amount of fiat currency in exchange for the same value of Ether.

How Does Ether Work?

New Ether are created through the process of mining. Every time a miner solves the mathematical problem associated with a block of transactions, five new Ether are created and rewarded to that miner. If another miner simultaneously finds a solution to the same block of transactions, he or she may be rewarded with two or three Ether (referred to as the aunt/uncle reward).

The Ether holds a crucial place in the Ethereum economy. Without it, the network would be unable to run because it fuels the apps and transactions that the network processes.

As a cryptocurrency, its uses outside of Ethereum are limited. Bitcoin can be used to buy and sell everyday goods, such as a cup of coffee or a bag of groceries. It is accepted by many large retailers, such as overstock.com and Microsoft, as well as a growing number of small businesses. It can even be used at some universities to pay for tuition! Ether, however, does not currently have those same uses. It is not accepted by retailers the way that Bitcoin is. This presents another crucial difference between Bitcoin and the Ether, or rather the mirror image of the fact that Bitcoin is not connected to any commodity while the Ether is. Bitcoin hit the mainstream partially because of its appeal as an alternative way to pay for everyday goods; if it couldn't be used by average people in their daily lives, it would have remained a fringe interest of the technophile community. The Ether was created for the simple (although not entirely exclusive) purpose of fueling the Ethereum network. Users must invest in the Ether and use it to pay for the transactions that they make. Therefore, its value is tied to how many people are using the Ethereum network. The growing number of people using Ethereum, combined with the sheer amount of money being invested by these people (and now large companies) in Ethereum projects is causing the value of the Ether to skyrocket. While the values of both Bitcoin and the Ether are connected to the laws of supply and demand, they operate for different purposes.

Think of Bitcoin as gold and the Ether as a diamond. Gold is a medium of exchange but has few purposes beyond that. It has no real industrial use, but its value tends to be quite high because people are willing to pay a lot of money for it. Gold jewelry is worth a lot because a lot of people want it; therefore, their higher demand attributes a higher value to it. Diamonds, on the other hand, are worth a lot on their own merit as a medium of exchange, but also have industrial use. They aren't only used in expensive jewelry, whose value is given to it based solely on how much people are willing to pay for it. They are also used in things such as saws and in procedures such as cutting, grinding, and polishing. Nothing is harder than a diamond, so diamonds have great use outside of being a medium of exchange.

Like gold, Bitcoin is not connected to a commodity. Its value is not based on any particular commodity but rather on how much people are willing to pay for it. The Ether, like a diamond, is worth a lot of money as a medium of exchange (it has grown in value over 4500% just in the first half of 2017), but it is more than that. It is what connects people to the Ethereum network and allows them to use it.

Chapter 5:

Applications on Ethereum

As previously explained, Ethereum powers a new kind of app, a decentralized application, referred to as a Dapp. This chapter will look at some of the Dapps that run on Ethereum, with the intent of giving you an idea of what kind of application is best suited to this platform.

Gnosis

Gnosis is a platform for making market predictions based on the consensus of a large group of people. This is referred to as crowd-sourced wisdom. For example, imagine that you ask a random person on the street who he thinks will win tonight's football game between the Horses and the Donkeys. That random person might not even know that there is a football game, and probably won't even care. However, if you got together hundreds or even thousands of people who are interested in football and are fans of one of the teams involved, the situation will be entirely different. Some of those fans may know their team's stats up and down the board and be able to accurately predict how well one team will fare (or not fare) against the other. With the wisdom of all those people combined, the odds of a successful prediction are significantly higher.

This principle of crowd-sourced wisdom is the idea behind Gnosis. Anyone can create an event, say, who will win the football game. Users of Gnosis can use their Gnosis tokens (whose value is set against the Ether) to make bets based on what they believe the outcome will be. The users who correctly predicted the outcome will divide the earnings between themselves.

Other than making money, the idea is to enable people to know in advance what will probably happen in the future, whether that be clear skies tomorrow or the stock market crashing.

FirstBlood

FirstBlood is what happens when the world of e-sports is connected to the power of a blockchain. Traditionally, the e-sports community is subject to a lot of regulation and corruption by the middlemen supposedly performing said regulation. There is also a lot of downtime, hacking, and problems with money transfers. FirstBlood aims to revolutionize e-sports by doing away with all of those problems.

Because of the secure blockchain network on which it operates. FirstBlood is not prone to hacking or any other security problems. Instead of betting with fiat currency through any traditional middleman, such as PayPal, bets are made in the token 1ST, the virtual currency of FirstBlood. The money is held in a smart contract until the winner of a match is declared. The money is then awarded to those who bet on the winner.

To make sure that the winner is reported accurately, FirstBlood randomly selects Witnesses from computer nodes on the network. The Witnesses are required to declare the winner and are compensated for their work. In order to become a Witness, individuals must submit a smart contract with a certain amount of 1ST tokens.

In the event of a disputed match, a Jury is selected from among those who watched the match. The Jurors report on who won the match and are compensated for their work. However, those who reported against what the majority determined may actually be penalized for false reporting.

Via FirstBlood, e-sports is becoming more transparent and free from the corruption that plagues the traditional industry.

Alice.SI

When deciding to donate to a charity, individuals are faced with the daunting task of determining whether or not a charity is legitimate. In the wake of catastrophes, such as Hurricane Katrina or the 2004 tsunami in Southeast Asia, false charities pop up to take advantage of the people who are ready and willing to give to those who are in desperate need. Now, with crowd-funding sites such as GoFundMe and Kickstarter, the problem is occurring at an even more grassroots level. Fraud on these websites runs rampant and is largely unchecked, so people end up inadvertently donating money to "causes" that are actually hoaxes. Some feel that this kind of fraud — taking money from kind-hearted people who are trying to give to those who are in need — has caused them to lose faith in humanity.

Enter Alice.SI. This Dapp was designed to provide accountability to charities by ensuring that they actually perform the work that they claim to do. When users want to donate to a charity but want to first confirm that it is legitimate, they can create a smart contract on Alice.SI, which will hold their funds until the charity in question proves that it has, in fact, done the work that it promised.

As you can probably see, applications on Ethereum are about engaging people as communities, which is reflective of the peer-to-peer structure of blockchain. People come together on these applications to engage in meaningful transactions with total transparency and without fear of corruption.

Chapter 6:

How to use Ethereum to Build an Application

This chapter will not get into all of the background knowledge required behind how to build an application, such as writing computer code or envisioning a concept for an app. It will rather give you an overview of the process involved in creating an application on Ethereum, which is different than creating apps on other platforms.

Before you can begin to turn your great idea into a Dapp, you need to become more familiar with the Ethereum network. You will probably want to look around at some Dapps to see what they do and how they work, to help you get an idea of what you want your Dapp to look like and how it should function. You will also want to look at different ways that people raised money for their Dapps, such as initial coin offerings (ICO's) and crowd-funding. You will also want to become a part of the blockchain community by joining chat rooms, blogs, and other forms of communication commonly used by those on blockchain. Making connections will not only help you raise money to fund your Dapp but will also put you in a better position for getting answers to the questions that will undoubtedly arise in the process of Dapp creation.

Will your Dapp be a type 1, type 2, or type 3? Remember that a type 1 is an entirely new blockchain, such as Bitcoin or Ethereum. That is probably too ambitious for your first Dapp, so you will want to make it either a type 2 or type 3. Type 2 Dapps are written onto the main blockchain, and Type 3 Dapps are built onto other pre-existing Dapps. Whichever one you decide will affect every step of the process.

Next, you will need to decide which programming language to use. Talk to people in the blockchain community to decide which programming language will be best. If you are more knowledgeable about one particular programming language, that will probably be the one that you will decide to use. However, there may be another programming language that is more suited to your Dapp. If that is the case, you will either need to become proficient in that programming language or hire someone who is. Keep in mind that one of the incentives behind the use of gas on Ethereum is to make the Dapps as efficient as possible. Inefficient, wasteful code costs more to execute, so while using a different programming language than what you are accustomed to may be difficult in the short-run, it will produce long-term benefits.

Then, you will need to decide on a framework to use. A framework supports the development of the application. Solidity, which was created for Ethereum, has two frameworks: Truffle and Embark. Truffle is the most popular framework. It a built-in compilation of smart contracts, which will be one of the central features of your Dapp. Embark allows for decentralized storage and decentralized communication; whether you choose to use Truffle or Embark will be based on your goals for your Dapp. Again, discussing which one will be best with members of the blockchain community will be in your best interest. You'll be talking with people who have already gone through this process and have the bruises to prove it. They will be able to share with you the wisdom they gained from their successes and failures. You will need to download and install the framework that you wish to use.

You will need to use the Ethereum home page (www.ethereum.org) to create a virtual currency on which your Dapp will run. The value of this virtual currency will be against the Ether (as opposed to the dollar or any other fiat or virtual currency) and will go up or down based on how successful your Dapp is. If you wish to hold an ICO to help raise money for the creation of your Dapp, you will need to have a strong proposal for what the Dapp will do and how it will work. Share this proposal with the blockchain community and see how much support you are able to get. You may have to invest some of your own money, but that doesn't mean your Dapp won't be successful.

Next is the intensive, time-consuming process of writing the code that will create and execute the Dapp. The code is incredibly important; anyone on the blockchain will be able to see it. The one heist that happened on Ethereum — that of the DAO in June of 2016 — happened hours after the Dapp was created because someone found a weakness in the code, which he exploited to siphon off tens of millions of dollars' worth of Ether. Because blockchain transactions are tamper-proof, the code cannot be changed. This means that if someone was to find a weakness in your code, you would only be able to sit back and helplessly watch all of the funds be depleted from your Dapp.

If you want to charge a transaction fee, that will probably need to be written into the initial code. Any other features, especially those generating income, will also need to be in the initial code, as the code cannot be changed.

Once the code is written, you will need to test out your Dapp in a sandbox. Using a sandbox will prevent the entire system from being affected should there be an error in your code. If you find any kind of weakness in it, you will be able to fix it without any financial or reputational repercussions (and in the world of Ethereum, reputational repercussions can be far worse than financial ones). Once you are satisfied with the code, have some technophile friends test it out. See if they are able to find a weakness in it that would be exploitable by someone on the blockchain.

Once your code is set and the Dapp is executable, it's time to launch it. Congratulations for achieving this milestone, and best of luck.

Chapter 7:

How to Make Money with Ethereum

Create a Dapp

One way to make money with Ethereum is to create your own Dapp. While the mechanics of how to create a Dapp involves the use of advanced computer coding, which is far beyond the scope of this ebook, this section will explain how a Dapp can generate income.

While your Dapp is in the process of being created (from your conception of the idea until it is released), you can generate money via a crowd sale. Ethereum has options for you to create your own virtual currency as part of your Dapp; you can hold an initial coin offering (ICO) in which people can invest in your virtual currency and, by extension, your Dapp. You can also launch a campaign on a site such as GoFundMe or Kickstarter to help fund your Dapp. The blockchain community tends to be extremely supportive, and some people have made millions of dollars off of it. They tend to want to help other people succeed, as well. Get your idea out to the community. Let people know that you are fully intent on making it work and that you have the competencies and resources (including time) required. And then see where that will take you.

Another way to make money via Ethereum Dapps is to charge a transaction fee. While in an ideal world we would be able to pursue our passions without having to worry about money, we live in a world in which money is essential to survival. Before you decide to charge a fee, you need to keep in mind two things. The first is that because Ethereum is an open-source blockchain, the information on it is not owned by anybody. Meaning that the information on your Dapp is not owned by you. The second thing to remember is that blockchain was created to put power back into the hands of the populace rather than in the hands of wealthy CEOs and the one percent. Don't become of the mindset that you will become like a wealthy CEO, or you will quickly lose the support of the blockchain community. Make your fees reasonable and as low as possible while still generating income for yourself. Because Ethereum Dapps run on smart contracts, every time a contract is made, the user sends a fee in Ether. You can opt to receive a cut of that fee.

A convenient way for both you and your users to make money off of your Dapp is to put ads on your Dapp. You will need to get businesses to agree to advertise on your Dapp for a certain amount of money each time the ad is viewed. Nobody likes having to watch ads (think of when a YouTube video gets interrupted by one), but what if your users could get paid for watching the ads on your Dapp? Give your users a share of the money generated from the ad and keep the rest for yourself. This feature alone could attract multiple new users to your Dapp, thereby increasing your income base.

There are other standard profit-generating strategies that have been used by traditional apps for years. They include charging a membership fee, charging a download fee, and paying for the services provided. One method that has been particularly successful is giving some basic version of the app for free; once users decide that they like it, they can pay to download the full version. All of the traditional methods for generating money on apps can be transferred to Dapps.

If coding is beyond your capabilities and interest, don't worry. There are still other ways that you can make money on Ethereum.

Mine on Ethereum

Becoming a miner on Ethereum is another way to generate income, as miners are rewarded with five Ether for each mathematical problem that they correctly solve. If the value of the Ether is at $300, then solving one of those problems will net you $1500! That is one way to pay off student loans.

There are two things that you will need in order to mine in such a way as to actually generate money. The first is an alternative energy source, such as solar or wind, to power your computer. Keep in mind that running a blockchain is extremely energy-intensive, and a lot of that energy is consumed from the process of mining. Using regular fossil fuel-powered electricity can actually make the mining process unprofitable because of how much you will pay in electricity costs.

The second thing that you will need is a computer outfitted with a graphics processing unit, or GPU, as even the most basic models of these run up to 200 times faster than a standard PC outfitted with a traditional CPU processor. A CPU processor is so inefficient that attempting to mine with it will be unprofitable.

Most mining computers are Windows-based, so the following guidelines are applicable to Windows. If you set up a Mac as a mining computer, you will probably need to tweak this information somewhat. You won't need to download the entire Ethereum blockchain onto your mining computer, which is great because it is over 20 gigabytes and growing! You will need to download a client, the mining app, and the Ethereum wallet.

Downloading the client will turn your computer into an Ethereum node and connect it to every other node on the Ethereum network. There are numerous clients that you can use; the most popular one, geth, runs on the command-line script Go. You will need to do some research to figure out which client is best suited for your knowledge base. In addition to connecting you to the Ethereum network as a node computer, the client will enable you to write smart contracts.

You will also need an Ethereum Mist wallet. You can easily find the wallet by searching online. It will download as a zip file; you will need to unzip and run it. Then, you will need to create an account so that you can send and receive Ether.

Next, you will need to download the mining app, Ethminer. Once Ethminer is installed, your computer will become part of the network that secures the Ethereum blockchain. You will also be able to begin mining.

There are two ways to mine. The first way is to go solo. Going solo means that you will have much less chance of solving the cryptographic puzzles necessary to win Ether, but whenever you do, you will get the entire payout. The other way is to join a mining pool. Mining pools combine the computational power of all of the users and split the payout equitably depending on how much power each user contributed. Miners who join mining pools tend to make more money, even though the payout on each solution is lower, because they are a part of so many more solutions. The number of members and amount of computational power that each mining pool has is constantly changing, so if you do join a mining pool, try to stay up to speed on the pool's stats.

Invest in the Ether

Another way to make money on Ethereum is to invest in the Ether. Cryptocurrencies are like traditional investments in many ways. You pay a dollar amount for the share (or in this case, the amount of Ether) that you want to buy. If the company (in this case, the Ethereum network) grows, then the value of the share, or Ether, grows, as well. Watch it grow your investment holdings.

There is one important distinction between investing in Ether and in traditional shares of a company: the rate at which the investment grows. Traditional investments may grow at a rate of two to three percent a year; growth of ten percent is considered rather high. The value of the Ether has grown by 4500 percent just in the first half of 2017! What that means for investors is if that rate of growth continues, instead of their money growing by maybe a paltry ten percent per year, it could grow by nearly 10,000 percent! There really is no easier way to make money.

Typically, high-yield investments are seen as risky; this principle is also true of cryptocurrency. Historically, cryptocurrencies have been subject to extreme volatility. The early years of Bitcoin saw periods in which its value would double in a matter of weeks, sometimes only in days, followed by a crash in which the currency would lose most of its value. Crashes were usually induced by massive thefts (like the infamous Mt. Gox heist that ultimately cost trillions of dollars and wiped out the holdings of thousands of Bitcoin investors).

However, security protocols for wallets that hold cryptocurrencies have increased tremendously, making security breaches a much more unusual phenomenon.

The major volatility of the Bitcoin market was also tied to the fact that, in its early days, not a lot of people used Bitcoin. Imagine a cannonball being dropped into a puddle of water. The entire system of water will be disrupted by the weight of the cannonball, simply because there is not much water present. However, if the same cannonball was dropped into an Olympic-sized swimming pool, it would create a relatively small splash, compared to the overall size of the pool. It might generate some small waves, but it wouldn't prove catastrophic to the pool the way that it would to the puddle. In the early days of Bitcoin when far fewer people were using the cryptocurrency, a theft was the equivalent of a cannonball being dropped into a puddle. Some, such as the Mt. Gox heist, proved to be nearly fatal to the entire Bitcoin community and nearly ended the run of virtual currency. However, now the Bitcoin community is so large that a large theft would be more like dropping a cannonball into an Olympic-sized swimming pool. Its effects would certainly be felt, but it wouldn't devastate the economy.

Ethereum has so many users who hold Ether that it is like the Olympic-sized swimming pool. In other words, even if a massive heist occurred, the felt impact would actually be quite small. There was a major crash that happened in the summer of 2017, following a rumor that Vitalik Buterin had died. The value of the Ether plummeted from approximately $300 to only about ten cents. However, it quickly regained its value and continued its upward trend of growth. All that is to say that while cryptocurrencies have historically been incredibly volatile, those wild swings are not nearly as wild or as frequent today.

Because the Ether is tied to a commodity — Ethereum — which is becoming increasingly popular and gaining traction even with multinational companies such as JPMorgan, demand for it, and with it its value, will probably continue to rise for the foreseeable future.

However, there is always a possibility that what some consider to be "the cryptocurrency experiment" will fail, causing investors to lose all of their holdings. A good rule of thumb is to only invest what you are willing to lose. Extra cash earned from a side gig, money that you saved by cooking at home instead of going out to eat, and a Christmas bonus from work are all good forms of income for investing in cryptocurrency. You probably won't starve or lose all of your retirement savings if the $50 that you earned mowing yards or shoveling snow went into the Ether before it crashed. You should not invest your retirement fund, your kid's college fund, or the money that you have saved for a down payment on a house in Ether or any cryptocurrency. If the market crashes, you will lose all of your holdings. Cryptocurrencies have consistently defied all of the dire predictions that economists have made, but this does not mean that they are invulnerable.

Another important investment decision is to diversify your portfolio, just like you would with a traditional investment. If you decide to invest in cryptocurrencies, invest in the Ether and in some other cryptocurrency, such as the LSK (which is connected to Lisk), Bitcoin, or LiteCoin. That way, if one currency should fail, you won't lose all of your holdings.

Conclusion

In conclusion, the potential that Ethereum has is limited only by the interests, talents, and capacities of the people who use it. As an open-source blockchain, none of the information on it is owned by any one person — not even its creator — but rather is shared by everyone on the network. This method of distributing information ensures that no one person is able to wield an incongruent amount of power or have leverage over others, which presents a drastic paradigm shift from the traditional concept of having a centralized governing body.

Vitalik Buterin envisioned that blockchain could be used for more than supporting the Bitcoin network, and his creation of Ethereum proved that this was true. Because of Ethereum, more and more people are able to access the benefits of blockchain, such as its transparent and trustless nature. One might even say that while Bitcoin created blockchain, Ethereum revolutionized it.

There are several ways that anyone with a computer and a little bit of know-how can generate income from Ethereum. One way is to create a Dapp and use any of the income-generating methods described in the last chapter. Another way is to mine for Ether, the virtual currency used to power the Ethereum network, and yet another way is to invest in Ether, as its value has soared exponentially.

Ethereum

Whatever you decide to do with Ethereum is entirely up to you. You may find that you are able to generate a steady stream of passive income, or maybe even find that you are its next overnight success story. The possibilities are limitless.